Songs from a Liverpool Childhood

A Narrative of Life in the Sixties

By
Phil Domingo
Illustrations
By Terry Elliott

First Published 2006 by Countyvise Limited,
14 Appin Road, Birkenhead, Wirral CH41 9HH.

Copyright © 2006 Philip Domingo

The right of Philip Domingo to be identified as the author of this work has been asserted by him in accordance with the Copyright, Design and Patents Act 1988.

British Library Cataloguing in Publication Data.
A catalogue record for this book is available from the British Library.

Please note: From 1st January 2007 ISBNs will contain 13 numbers these numbers will be the same as the present number printed below the barcode (ie. starting 978). Countyvise is showing both existing (10 digit) and future (13 digit) ISBNs on the Title page verso. Please continue to use the 10 figure number until 31st December 2006.

ISBN 1 901231 77 1   ISBN 978 1 901231 77 9

'I think if you enjoy a childhood it is indelible for life'
Spike Milligan

In The Beginning

In 2001 my cousin Bob, known in these pages as Robert, sent me a copy of the Liverpool F. C. fanzine 'Red All Over The Land', open at a page where there was a poem called 'The Old Boy's Pen' by Dave Kirby. I was totally 'blown away' by this. Its detail, its accuracy and all round brilliance immediately struck a chord. I too had watched Liverpool from the children's enclosure at Anfield overseen by my dad in the Kop as he passed food through to me and Robert.

I had always wanted to write but wondered what to write about. There it was in front of me in stark simplicity, 'write about what you know and understand.' The thing I understood best was football. A few months later, the Liverpool footballing legend Billy Liddell passed away. Given that he was my father's absolute hero, in fact obsession would not be an exaggeration, it opened up a lot of latent grief over my dad who had died six years earlier. Just then a song appeared in my head,' When I was born in 'fifty-five the greatest hero then alive' and the poem 'Boots of Thunder' was born. It fronts as a tribute poem to Billy but is really about my dad. I submitted it tentatively to the fanzine and to my astonishment they printed it.

That gave me the confidence to continue. I then proceeded to write tribute poems to my own footballing heroes and had more success in terms of publication in the fanzine. I wrote some retro articles and poems too.

One day I was thinking of my happy childhood spent with my cousin in the 'River' streets of Toxteth and I wrote 'Street Kings' which opens and sums up this collection. It did not get printed in the fanzine because although it alludes to football, it is about childhood.

I had crossed over. Some more time elapsed until one evening when, like so many parents to-day, I was chauffeuring my children from dancing to cricket etc., I thought how very different this all is to my experience. How very safe, sanitised and orchestrated their childhood is compared to mine. No play stations then just an old tin can, a 'frido' ball and a wheel and a stick.

Not that my childhood could compare to the real poverty and danger of that of say, my dad in the thirties and early forties, but enough time had elapsed for the sixties to become History itself. So I decided to build on 'Street Kings' and put a collage together of life in those streets from the perception of an eight year old with the hindsight of an adult.

I decided to write about the games we played, and the things that happened both joyous and tragic. l have attempted to bring back to life the characters, mostly upright folk and also one or too dodgy ones (although we didn't realise it at the time). How important in the eyes of a child is the person who sells sweets and fish and chips. The shopkeepers were the 'medieval barons' of these streets.

I have tried to acknowledge Liverpool's seafaring history and that our neighbourhood was a living war museum - they still hadn't fully cleared up after the blitz - I have referred to the ongoing effect that bombing had on the likes of my mother.

I thought I'd write about schooldays. What I did not expect was the torrent of Catholicism which to quote Dylan was 'pouring out onto every page like it was written in my soul'. I thought I'd moved on but it's still there.

I have paid tribute to the importance of all of my family – the Domingos and the Troys - most of whom lived in the adjoining streets. That's something else my own children have missed out on. I have used these family members to convey a detail or an attitude from the time.

I have tried to capture not just a place but a time . My parents were so deeply affected, as was everybody, by the tragedies at Aberfan and Saddleworth Moor that here I grieve for my contemporaries - my generation.

Yes the Beatles get a mention but also the 'Demons of Dartford' too and of course 'Thunderbirds and the 'Boys of '66'. Time as well as place.

Why 'Songs' not 'poems'? As an English graduate I believe that poetry requires additional characteristics other than a rhyming pattern. One or two have these features and are proper poems but the rest are songs or rhythms in my head. Now if any one out there wants to put these to music – 'Songs- the Musical?' – I'd love to hear from you.

If this strikes a chord with you because you were in that place or that time or both, or even if you had an exciting childhood, please let me know.

I hope you have as much enjoyment reading them as I did writing them.

Phil Domingo, August 2006-08-14

philip. domingo9@ntlworld. com

The Writer

Phil Domingo lives in Northampton where he has taught French for the last twenty-six years. He is married with two teenage children but nevertheless professes to be happy. Presently he is an Assistant Principal at Kingsthorpe Community College Northampton. He still maintains strong links with his native city where so many of his family still live. He is definitely on the Red side of the divide but hopes this book will be read by all creeds because it's about childhood and we all have one of those.

The Illustrator

Terry 'Tee-Gee' Elliott
The venerable Barovian is a friend and former colleague. Terry taught Art, Design and Technology for many years and has a background as a draughtsman. To get him to do this he had to be dragged kicking and screaming from retirement, where he was suffering from a serious overdose of dotage on his grand-daughters.

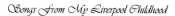

For Robert (Bob to his mates).
You're like a cousin to me!

Street Songs

Street Kings

Toxteth boys,
Kings of the street
Ran through the jiggers, *
Ball at our feet

Ruined our school shoes
Kicked out the toes.
In one-a-side matches,
Where anything goes.

Thousands of headers
Against a school wall (St. Bernards Kingsley
Road)
Repetitive pounding
Of an old "Frido" ball.

From sun up to sundown
We'd gleefully play
We were St John or Roger
Till the end of the day.

The solitary respite
When energy dipped
Was to go round to Comers' (Alt street)
For a big bag of chips
("put two pies in please Sarah")

Then round to Bob Cook's
The shop on Exe Street (corner)
Four Walkers (toffees)a penny
Our favourite sweet.

* Jiggers - Back alleys

"Pay your own China"
If windows were broke. . .
"It wasn't me mister
It was some other bloke. "

The game lasts forever
Or at least till your dad
Came down to fetch you
"Your mum's going mad!"

Then it's over to Anfield
When Saturday came.
We'd queue for the bus
By the Baths in Lodge Lane,
And the queue for the "Special"
Went down Beaumont Street
(round past the library)
All to see Peter Thompson's
Wondrous feet.

Compulsory purchase
Posters went up.
The bulldozers came.
And the streets that we loved
Were reduced to rubble
Where communities thrived
'Cos somebody thought
That we kids were deprived.

Deprived with the Beatles ?
Deprived with the Stones ?
And Thunderbirds on
The telly at home.
You could see your Grandparents

At the end of the street
And get tea and hot toast
And a shilling a week

A World Cup for Roger
A man on the moon
And ever was Anfield
In glory festooned

We wanted for nothing
Our families made sure
Security, love and great warmth
Were in store.
Whole extended families
Were split up for good
To Hough Green and Garston
Speke and Halewood.

Whole Sundays were wasted
For buses we'd wait
To visit grandparents
On some distant estate.

It needn't have happened
A solution was there
To build on the bathrooms
Where the old shelters were(in the back-
yards)

Once inseparable cousins,
When rarely we meet
We long for the days
When we were kings of the streets.

Song for Harold

refrain
Harold put those matches down
They're bound to cause alarm
Your life is precious don't you see
You don't deserve such harm

As smoke poured out from a Thames Street
home
The neighbours were distraught
"She's got two kids in that blazing house "
As firemen bravely fought

The mother threw the baby down
To safe and thankful arms
Then leapt herself and broke her fall
But still she was alarmed

" I can't find Harold please help me
I think he's still downstairs"
As Harold hid behind the couch
No one was aware

My uncle Jack went round the back
A rescue was his aim
But climbed down from his ladders
Defeated by the flames

Distressed and broken was poor Jack
A life he tried to save
It was little consolation
That the neighbours thought him brave

When the firemen did break through
Alas it was too late
They found poor Harold age just six
The smoke had sealed his fate

Now Harold liked excitement
He loved to play with fire
He crept downstairs and struck a match
Disaster did transpire

His final moments all alone
The frightened boy did choke
Sobbing loudly for his mum
Submerged in flames and smoke

And all the neighbours wept with grief
And felt the pain within
As silence fell on Thames Street
With faces bleak and grim

The whole of Toxteth filled the streets
Upon the funeral day
You couldn't move in Alt Street
As the cortege made its way

A little boy my childhood friend
I remember clearly now
A needless death a page still blank
I wonder why and how

Refrain

Neighbourhood Bully Song

He was the toughest kid in Toxteth
Yet no one saw him fight
Short and round with a big flat head
He was a fearsome sight
He'd make you all 'a quiver from your head
down to your feet
Let's go and hide let's go inside 'cause
Scon'ead's in our street

He ruled by reputation
The fear that he would
And all the kids believed it
Throughout the neighbourhood
There's a figure on the corner we don't want
to draw the heat
Let's go and hide let's go inside 'cause
Scon'ead's in our street

I heard he beat a kid up once
By ripping off his head
"He really hates the Catholic kids
He'd like to see them dead"
You hear the bones a shaking and the chat-
tering of the teeth
Let's go and hide let's go inside 'cause
Scon'ead's in our street

He had a little brother
Much younger than old Scon
He'd shoot his mouth off all the time
And threaten with "our John"
No children's games no kick the can no foot-

ball teams to beat
Let's go and hide let's go inside 'cause
Scon'ead's in our street

He wasn't scared of coppers
I heard he'd give them hell
They'd try to apprehend him
And he battered them as well
With muscles made of granite stones and a
head made of concrete

Let's go and hide let's go inside yes Scon'eads
in our street

The Penny Man

There was a kind old man in a derelict flat
 Which he shared with many mice and rats
"If he offers you sweets you don't take any"
The grown ups disliked Mr Penny

He was a kind old man in an old brown mac
He smiled at the kids and we smiled back
He made us laugh he was dead funny
And if you asked him he would give you
money

He was a kind old man and we knew him
well
His clothes were old with a dirty smell
We remember to this very day
When they took the Penny Man away

The Fugitive

There was a one armed man in Sixby's shop
On his withered limb he wore a sock
And if his cat made a mess he'd use it as a
mop
Then serve you lolly ices enough to put you
off

Now the 'Fugitive' was on the box
Did the murderer wear an old blue sock?
It would give Richard Kimble quite a shock
To find the one armed man in Sixby's shop

Gambling Song

Every Sunday lunchtime at the bottom of Thames
Street
The men they empty from the pub and gather round
to meet
They always wear their Sunday best, they're wearing
suits and ties
Their hair is 'Brylcreemed, to a quiff above their
bleary eyes

They toss a penny in the air and have a little bet
They guess the outcome of the toss and then begin to
sweat
The crowd becomes excited their faces red and
bright
The game is known as pitch and toss, the slang is
'Heads and S###'

Soon the money changes hands to joy and great
despair
Sometimes it is a ten bob note and half crowns here
and there
A police car turns into the street and panic grips the
men
We see the dissolution of the outdoor gambling den

Bonfire Song

It's the middle of October and the feeling is
so good
We're gonna raid a derelict house and collect
some 'Bommy wood'
Our 'bommy' will be brilliant, it will be the
best
Higher than the houses, you can forget the
rest

We're gonna need a 'steerie' with a decent set
of wheels
We'll load the doors on carefully so the
steerie doesn't squeal
I've got me mother's stockings to make a
decent guy
I'll fill it with news paper and the pennies
they will fly

It's the middle of October and it's well
understood
That every kid in Liverpool is collecting
'bommy' wood

Steerie = go cart with old pram wheels
Bommy= bonfire

Lament for Eddie

Eddie was only six when his mother left home. His dad was left to bring up Eddie and his two teenage brothers. In those days it was highly unusual for either parent to leave the family home let alone a mother

Eddie's dad was a bus driver who worked shifts. Obviously a caring man - his boys loved him to bits - but it's not always easy for a dad to fill a mother's role. When dad was at work Eddie was left to his own devices. Often he would wander the streets eating his hallmark brown sauce 'butty'. He was a real 'Daddy's' boy.

The mothers in the streets felt really sorry for Eddie and would often take him in and give him a good feed. Very often he would have the run of an empty house .... and so did we.

Robert and I and the gang would often hang out in Eddie's causing all kinds of mischief and no little damage. One time an impromptu game of cricket led to Robert swinging the bat through the front room bay window. Glass was everywhere. Eddie's dad went mad.

We could gain access to Eddie's house even when Eddie wasn't there. There was a coal cellar underneath the hall which led to a flight of stairs up to the kitchen. The cellar was accessible via a manhole cover in front of the doorstep.

How did we, Eddie's 'friends' support him in these circumstances? Answer ..... We made it worse, took advantage and bullied him. That is the nature of some children to our eternal shame. One evening, late in the summer holidays of the year when

England won the (football) world cup. Robert devised a cunning plan.

'We'll get into Eddie's coal cellar, make spooky noises and frighten the life out of him'.

'Great idea Rob, let's do it. We need to find out if Eddie's dad's in or not'.

'Right Phil. You go and find out and if he is, you go first down the manhole, followed by Alan Forrester. I'll come down later.
So I knocked on the door. 'Eddie is your dad in?
'No he's at work'
'Thanks. See ya.'
I walked back to Robert.
'It's all clear. Let's go. '

I climbed down into the cellar and sat on the coal. There were spiders and cobwebs everywhere. It was filthy and very scarey. Alan started to climb down. Just then there was a terrific roar and the thunderous sound of footsteps running down the stairs. At that moment Alan's legs shot up from the hole and the cover slid over to shut out what little light there was. Blackness was everywhere. The others had escaped and I was left alone trapped as Eddie's dad stood on the manhole cover. 'Philip Domingo. I know it's you down there. Where's that Robert Hughes? It's him I want . '

Huh. I don't know Mr. J. Please let me out I'm scared. I promise never to do it again.' I sobbed. I was down there for an age begging and pleading. Eventually Mr J. opened the manhole cover and hoisted me up.
'Right we're off to the Police Station in Kingsley Road'.

'Oh please Mr J. I didn't mean it'.
Just then Auntie Elsie was crossing Alt Street towards us, in her slippers.

' Ted let him go. I'll sort this out. None of us need any more trouble'.

'Elsie we've had enough of him and your Robert'.
'Leave it to me Ted. It won't happen again'.

And it never did. Elsie saved the day.

As we walked past Lydiate Street, two figures could be seen. Weaving in and out of the bay windows. One had a shock of blond hair - my cousin Robert.

The punishments were severe - a good grounding for the Catholic Grammar school I was about to attend. Robert and I often talk about this episode when Auntie Elsie got us out of a fix. I last saw Eddie in 1971 after he had joined the army. He was happy and seemed to be well suited to army life. He was no pushover then and there was no sign of a 'sauce butty'.

Song for the Axing

Alf Laver was the oldest man that you could wish to meet
He used to chop up firewood at the bottom of our street
He'd chop it into twelve inch strips with deadly accuracy
And tie it into bundles and sell it off you see

His axe was sharp as it could be his aim was ever good
His shop was sparse and spartan with the smell of firewood
His backyard wall was made secure with broken glass on top
In case we might bunk over and steal his precious stock

His goods would burn in every home throughout the
neighbourhood
And every house in Toxteth used Laver's firewood
You'd think he'd be a rich man, the type who chewed the fat
But he dressed like old man Steptoe without the bowler hat

Now we would play our football games outside of Alfie's
shop
And sometimes break his windows, which happened quite a
lot
Then we would scarper quickly, mindful of the fact
 That Alfie Laver might be old but he's handy with an axe

Sweet Song

Walker's toffees me favourite sweet
The staple diet around Exe Street
Four for a penny a load for a bob
Buy 'em in a bag from Bob Cook's shop

It's Friday night and we're showing willing
For pocket money-we'll get a shilling
Then it's down to Bob's for a weekly treat
A paper bag full of Walker's sweets

Jumping Doorsteps

Jump the airies*, jump them fast
Jump all day let's make it last

Jump one skip one
Change a leg
Jump until it's time for bed

Leap a doorstep then try two
When there's nothing else to do

Jump one skip one
Change a leg
Jump until it's time for bed

Beat your record as you leap
Jumping until it's time to sleep
Jump the airies jump them fast
Jump all day let's make it last

Jump one skip one etc.

*Airies are the raised concrete bedding for perimeter railings
which went round a bay window of the terraced houses
and separated doorsteps. The railings were removed for
munitions during World War Two leaving a low flat parapet
to run and leap along.

Street Moaner

Google-eye hated football but he hated children more
And he would always chase us when we played outside his door
" Get lost, clear off " he would shout "Go and play elsewhere
And take that blinking ball with you, " and he began to swear
"Go to the park, play in your street, just don't play here at all
I'll put a flippin' knife through it if I catch that flippin' ball

News got out that Google-eye was moving in due course
And all the kids in Thames Street cheered till they were hoarse
"Google-eye's off in the morning" you'd hear the children cry
Now we can play outside his house, "Oh Google-eye Good bye"

Collector's items

Lolly ice sticks all over the ground
Lolly ice sticks are there to be found
Collect them and keep them
They dirty your hands
Show to your mates
But don't tell your Mam

Lolly ice sticks so good to collect
Lolly ice sticks I like to inspect
Pick them up from the gutter
Pick them up from the floor
But don't tell your mother
Or the woman next door

Our Street

Our street's the best 'cos we're all hard
Our street's the best and our back yard
We've got the best airies we've got the best
lights
We have the best bommies on bonfire night

Our street's the best because we live there
Our street's the best and we don't care
We've got the best neighbours
We've got the best kids
We've got the best dustbins and best dustbin
lids

Our street's the best because unlike yours
We scrub the steps at our front doors (well
our mams do)
We've got the best jiggers we've got the best
dogs
We've got the best exterior bogs

Gravity Song

Raymond Raymond
Please don't try
Batman really cannot fly
Nor can Robin not a bit
This is dangerous don't try it

Raymond Raymond
Please don't jump
On your head you'll have a lump
If you don't climb down from that wall
You'll lose your footing you may fall

Raymond Raymond
Please don't leap
You're bound to make your mother weep
A caped crusader he maybe
But he can't defy gravity (and neither can
you)

Walking the Walls at Midnight

It is the midnight hour and nothing stirs at all
It is the perfect time at night to walk the backyard walls
I go down to the kitchen then I turn the key
I'm out there in the backyard now, unsupervised and free
I bunk up on the mangle and then onto the wall
There's no one around to help me, if I should ever fall

The moon shines on the rooftops, the neighbourhood is still
Apart from a boy who walks the walls to get some kind of
thrill
The cats are climbing drainpipes not bothered by this lad
Who thinks that he is spiderman, he's obviously mad
A light is on across the way in a kitchen in Thames Street
A woman peers through the curtains, why does she never
sleep?

'I saw your boy out late again, walking the backyard walls
It would be very dangerous if he were to take a fall'

 'I swear you must be seeing things, you need to check your
sight
 My children they were tucked in bed entirely through the
night'

In years to come I told my mum about the times I climbed
the walls
She wasn't very happy, she wasn't pleased at all

'I told that woman all that time that she must be off her head
As you were risking life and limb while we were all in bed'

Song for Friendly Edna

Now Edna's very friendly
My mother used to say
She has a lot of visitors
Throughout the night and day
And all the kids look different
With different coloured hair
But still they are related
And they don't really care

Yes Edna's good to everyone
And everybody knew
Different cars outside the house
Some red some green some blue
And all the kids look different
With different coloured eyes
That really doesn't bother them
You have to realise

Hey mum you could be friendly too
If only now and then
And we'd get lots of presents
From lots of different men
Do you really want that Philip?
Do you really want that lad?
No man on earth could give you
What you get from your dad

Different dads different dads
Must be great to have different dads

Song For A Local Hero

The message "Welcome Home Ken" was written on a wall
And we all wondered who Ken was, who he was at all
He could have been a soldier returning from the war
A Liffey Street hero? I wish we knew the score

His family clearly missed him, not difficult to see
I wondered what was his part in the Allied victory?
Was he a fighter pilot, a hero in a plane?
He might have been at Anzio or at El Alamein

I wondered where he might have lived, if he was still alive
And why the message still survived in nineteen sixty-five
I wondered about the party the family might have had
To celebrate the return of their soldier hero lad

Along with missing houses from which there's no escape
The message was a feature of an after war landscape
I wondered all about it, I'm sure I'm not alone
I'd like to join the chorus of "Kenneth Welcome Home"

Chippy Song

Refrain
Comer's chips just can't be beat
Crisp and salty great to eat

Tommy Comer's chipshop was the best in L'pool 8
Everybody went there to taste the food so great
The fish he sold were battered till they were nearly dead
Tommy was a cheerful man with a very shiney head

'Yaze' Tommy was a pleasant man who loathed to disagree
'Yaze' he'd say to everything apart from 'credit please'
Now we would try to get him to say the odd catchphrase
Like 'Put the pies in Sarah followed by a 'Yaze'

'The shop's on fire Tommy' this cheeky boy would say
'Sarah put the pies in and chase that boy away'
And every Saturday lunchtime we'd always lick our lips
'Here's two bob, go do a job and fetch some Comer's chips'

Transport Song

Once I had a stick then I had a wheel
Do want to know how good that feels?
I'd truck it up and down all day
While other kids would watch and play
I'd wheel it up and down the street
And save the wear upon my feet

And then one day I got it nicked
Had no wheel I'd just a stick
The consequence filled me with dread
I'd have to walk around instead!

Cheeky Song

Small children often play a game
"If I cover my eyes I become invisible".

Hansen had a grocer's store on the corner of a street,
And we would often go there to buy a bag of sweets,
There were big sacks of potatoes upon the concrete floor,
He was always pleased to see us when we walked through
the door,
He was a proper gentleman and very amply fed,
And I swear he had a little (egg board) lion stamped upon
his shiney head,
And I would often comment upon his egg-shaped dome,
"That cheeky boy needs to be taught some manners in the
home",

Our friend's dad parked his taxi outside old Hansen's store,
And we climbed in to shout rude things at the grocer
through the door,
We knew we'd be invisible behind the tainted glass,
How could we be identified unseen but heard alas

The Rolling Stones had a record out "It's all over now",
And we adapted lyrics which seemed to fit some how,

"He used to wake in the morning, Mr Hansen in bed,
I wouldn't worry but he's got a shiney head, and now he's
hairless up there and balding all around, got an egg board
lion stamped upon his shiney crown".

"Philip and Robert, I know it's you, I can tell by your voices,
what will I do?

I'll go to your parents and ask them to stop, sending their boys along to my shop".

My father wasn't very happy and a price I had to pay, I wasn't allowed to go outside, not allowed to play (for a week)

Wash Day Song

I'm going to the wash house
I'm going with me mam,
We're taking all the washing
In me little sister's pram.

And all the wash house women
Are there to do the chore,
With head scarves tied and pinnies on
And bare arms to the fore.

The wash house will be rumbling
With the noises of the machines,
And the hall it will be steaming
As they scrub the washing clean.

And all the latest gossip
Is churned out as they try
To stop "their dirty washing"
Being hung outside to dry.

And when the washing's clean and dry
I go back with me mam,
And no doubt find another use
For my little sister's pram.

A Flemish Painter from the Middle Ages visits

Peter Breughel (the elder) came to our street,
"Lean your easel against that telegraph pole and paint away
Pete"
That's old Pat – he's a bit Flemish too judging the way he
coughs his guts up each morning,
And there's me mum and Mona and Vera having a chat
over something and nothing,
While I wait for your mum to open the front door
"Don't interrupt Philip, it's rude"
"But mum I'm bursting"
Old Ma' Ecc. is keeping watch from her door step,
"Mind where you put that easel, my husband fought
foreigners like you in the war"
Her daughter chimes in "No we don't like to go on holiday as
Jack did enough travelling in the army".

"Hansen's put his prices up again a loaf will soon be two
bob you watch better off going to Bob Cooke's (shop) or the
(Lodge) Lane.
Children swing from a rope thrown over a black lamp post,
Two boys kick a plastic ball, in a one-a-side shooting match,
Two girls run in desperation towards an old tin can,
Others hide in jiggers or behind bay windows
or behind the only two parked cars in the street,
A grey Ford Popular and a white Zephyr
"The door to number 18 is rusty maroon not red Peter"

Two girls play house on a front door step
"Isn't the potty a bit too realistic?"
The girls then run off to stroke the ragman's horse,
While others trade in an old mangle for a plastic flying bird,
A woman in an apron kneels to scrub her door step spotless,
A strange boy rotates an old pram wheel with a stick,
"Better than walking pal"
Girls play two balls against a wall,
Skirts tucked under so they can jump over the balls,
Other children engage in games of bulldog and re-alleyo.

Two boys strum plastic Beatles guitars
while wearing plastic Beatles wigs,
Others race tri-cycles up and down the street
One boy's "steerie" is now a go-kart
his dad has helped him – the cheat.
"Nearly done Peter?"
When you've finished painting the street
you can white wash our back yard wall.

Footnote: When Breughel the younger came to paint our
street years later it had been demolished.

On Horseback

Run round the jiggers as if you're on a horse
Slapping your buttocks with considerable
force
Do it like Lone Ranger or do it like Tonto
'Hit it Kemo Sabi, Silver lad Hi Ho

Dodging round the dogmuck like a slalem
skier
When you're riding Silver you never have a
fear
Ride him on a prairie ride him north and
south
Ride him on the debris of an old bombed
house

Kick the Can

Refrain

Kick the can, kick the can
Fix the dip so you're not 'man'
Come and find us if you can
Let's have a game of kick the can

The Dip

Dip dip dip my blue ship, sailing on the water
like a cup and saucer
O. U. T spells out

On winter days and summer nights
In the middle of our street
We'd place a can on a tarmac line
And play some hide and seek

The rules

You'd throw the can for the one who's 'man'
While others went and hid
In jiggers and in doorways
Or behind a dustbin lid
And if the 'man' did spot you
A race then did ensue
To reach the can before the 'man'
So the new 'man' wasn't you
It was an understanding

That no one strayed too far
That hiding places were reached on foot
And not by bus or car

One summer's day we fixed the dip
So Johnny B. was 'man'
Then Robert then concocted
A very cunning plan
'We'll catch a bus from Parly Street
And go to Pier Head

So Johnny spent the afternoon
Befuddled and bemused
While so called friends
Smoked old dog ends
And smirked about their ruse
Eventually we both turned up
With no sign of our 'man'
Sent to bed without his tea
And cursing 'Kick the Can'

Debris Song

Go to the debris that's where we play,
That's where we spend most of the day,
Kick an old ball, throw a tin can,
Hide in the shelter from the old Penny Man,
Play on the debris, run on the mound,
Unearth a brick that's lodged in the ground,
Dig out a drain pipe, frighten a mouse,
Smash all the windows in the derelict house,
Swing round a lamp-post, tie round your
coat
So three of you swing on an old piece of
rope,
We don't need a swing park; we don't need a
slide,
We know where to run and we know where
to hide
(apologies to Martha Reeves)
Go to the debris that's where we play,
That's where we spend most of the day.

Library Song

"Go to the library, read all day,
Let imagination take you away".

In Lodge Lane there's a library
Where you can borrow books,
It won't cost you a penny
So why not take a look.

It's spacious and it's peaceful
And no one's in a rush,
With a couple of librarians
Who order you to hush.

I go there with my mother
Every other week,
It's something to look forward to
Although you're not allowed to speak.

I'll read about Brer Rabbit
And then the 'Secret Seven',
My mind it wanders far and wide
I'm in a reader's heaven.

I hand my ticket to the man
Who's very nice indeed,
I'm really very happy
That I've been taught to read.

"Go to the library, read all day,
Let imagination take you away".

Shoe Song(a dilemma)

Robert and I had a Frido Ball
With Stanley Matthews' name upon
We'd take it out and play all day
He, Roger Hunt, me, Ian St John

We always had a shooting match
At the bottom of our street
And kick that ball with all our might
Till we had blisters on our feet

This would drive our mothers mad
 Maternal tempers they would lose
The sisters in unison would say
'We can't afford to replace your shoes'

To this we were oblivious
And off we went to play
Another one a side shooting match
Through the entire day

One day our Robert hit a shot
Which sailed right through the air
And went through Laver's window
Glass was everywhere

Through the jigger he did run
Our Robert moved at pace
Leaving me out on my own
Alf Laver now to face

'Oh Alf I know who did it'
I meekly volunteered
And grassed my cousin Robert up
The watching kids just jeered

'He's gone and grassed his cousin up
 What kind of cousin he?
To risk the family honour
For a bout of honesty'

Many adults felt the same
And I became confused
Because all I did was tell the truth
And now I stand accused

Three of Us ?

In Jupiter Street (unadopted) we parked
our car (c. 1967)
And boys appeared from near and far.
"Can I mind it Mister, there'll be no catch.
It will still be here after the match. "

We'd start to walk the golden mile,
Excitement building all the while.
We'd dodge the cars at Breck Road lights,
The road to Anfield in our sights.

And so we're now on Walton Breck,
And past the big pub on the left.
A father walking with his lad
The proudest time for any dad.

We see the signs for Walker's Ales,
The smell of onions now prevails.
The step now quickens, pulses race.
Fortnightly ritual taking place.

By now the road it straightens out,
Souvenir sellers all about.
And desperate fellows here and there,
Asking if "there's any spares?"

Pedestrian traffic all one way,
To Anfield on a big match day.
And behold it's Mecca, eyes aloft.
The silver roof of Spion Kop.
Volume rises on our approach,

More fans arrive by bus, by coach.
We plan to meet at the D:E:R (telly shop)
Then separate and say "tara ".

Dad takes his seat in the Kemlyn Road.
I make for the Pen, but he'll never know,
That I'll sneak to the Kop, unless I get hurt,
And get passed down to sit on the dirt.

And after the match once more we'd meet,
And make our way back to Jupiter
Street(unadopted).
He'd ask some questions, he'd ask a lot,
He'd ask me about the view from the Kop.

35 years later. . . . .

I make that journey from time to time,
Now I'm the dad and the lad is mine.
But I feel a presence in my bones,
And sense that we don't walk alone.

In the centenary stand . . . .

The turnstile clicks for only two,
But could it be that we know who
Has come to join us – quite discreet,
As we sit near his former seat?

*Old Kopites never die they just float around
Anfield on match days.*

Member Song

It's the General Election of 1964
And all the hopeful candidates are knocking
on the door
There's one called Bessie Braddock the nicest
one so far
She gave me and Rob a ride in a chauffeur
driven car

At first she introduced herself, she said she's
our M. P.
My dad approves of Bessie because 'She
stands for us you see'
We showed her Comer's chippy our favourite
take away
And then to Alt Street debris that's where we
like to play

I said I liked her chauffeured car, 'It's really
rather good'
And added 'This'd come in handy for collecting bommy wood'
And so the ride came to an end and we all
said 'tara'
I hope she gets elected and can keep the
groovy car

Walk in the Park

"Let's leave home" our Robert said
"I've got ten woodbines here
You don't need food when you've got fags"
And we all said "hear hear"

"Let's all go to Sefton Park
And find a wooded glen
We'll live there without grown ups
And there create a den"

We wandered through the winding streets
Until we reached Lodge Lane
We were down to only six cigarettes
As we walked in the rain

We went up to the Palm House
But we couldn't find a glen
It was not a bit like Robin Hood
Wet kids not merry men!

We walked past Peter Pan's statue
And marched onto the lake
We walked around the lakeside
It was a big mistake

The lakeside stones were treacherous
Then Robert cried "Oh hell"

We all watched with horror
As Tommy slipped and fell

"The little fella's in the lake"
I heard our Robert shout
Then we all went to lend a hand
And sought to pull him out

We all grabbed poor Tommy
And pulled him from the lake
Freezing cold and soaking wet
The child began to shake

'I didn't want to come here
I didn't want to come
Robert, Philip, take us home
I want my dad and mum'

'Tommy stop your crying
You silly little fool
We're on a big adventure
We're off to Otterspool'

As the merry band marched on
Towards the promenade
We saw that in the distance
Some men were running hard

Upon this realisation
We started turning back
These men were no one other
Than me dad and Uncle Jack

'You are for it now my lad
Your mother's in a state
You're all in trouble all of you
Let's go it's getting late'

Eventually we all got home
And I was sent to bed
With nothing more than a glass of milk
And a plain white slice of bread

Family Songs

Sibling Song

Sisters sisters they're no fun
They can't play football climb or run
They can only skip and play two balls
They're really not much fun at all

"A baby brother's what I need"
"No chance another mouth to feed?
Kids cost money don't you know
And your dad works at the G. P. O"
"But the people in the older flats
 Are really poor and that's a fact
And they have babies all the time
I want a brother to call mine"
"But they're good Catholics and they pray
To baby Jesus every day"

So one day after school I went
To St Bernard's church during Lent
I went down on my bended knees
"Give me a brother Jesus please"
My parents searched most everywhere
For a missing son consumed in prayer
"Have you seen Philip he's not yet home
He's an hour late and all alone"
Then mother guessed where I might be
In a place of holy sanctuary
She remembered that I once did mention

The need to seek some intervention
And so they found me in the church
Relieved to terminate the search

Sisters sisters they're no fun
They can't play football climb or run ?
They only skip and play two balls
They're really not much fun at all

Sofa Song

When he had no money for a bet
Me Grandad had the best plan yet
He'd lift the couch up from the ground
And turn the whole thing upside down
There was never ever any doubt
That all the coins would roll on out
And Grandad's face betrayed a smile
As all the coins became a pile
I would like now to endorse
It seemed a kingdom for a horse
The horse's name-it's not a shock
'Sofa(r) so good' in the two o'clock

Uniform Song

My dad was in the Royal Marines
But now he lives at home
I've searched the house most everywhere
But can't find his trombone

My dad was in the Royal Marines
And served in Palestine
' Keep on polishing your shoes
Till you see your face like mine'

My dad was in the Royal Marines
And sailed around Cape Horn
But now he is a postman
He's back in uniform

My dad was in the Royal Marines
I knew respect and fear
So I became a rebel
In my later teenage years

My dad was in the Royal Marines
He never played trombone
And I preferred the Rock and Roll
Played by the Rolling Stones

My dad was in the Royal Marines
And that can't be so bad
One day I'll join the Royal Marines
And be just like my Dad

Please Let me join the
Marines when I growup
well I am only 7 nour
wood you Let me come
every Tuesday whenI am
15 Master PhilLip Doringo
18 Exe st Liverpool8 my
Father Mr vicent Domingo
has allready joind the
Marins

War Child

One day in 1941
My mother woke her best friend gone,
In years to come it caused her trouble
To see her friend pulled from the rubble,
She talked about it constantly
Prayed on her mind incessantly.

And, after in those war torn years
In an air raid shelter filled with fear,
A family spent the nights forlorn
Wondering would they see the dawn,

One night a flare fell in the yard
And Uncle Bobby threw it hard,
Away to safety in the street
Collective hearts all missed a beat.

No more a target for the bombs
Which fell in 1941.

Post Natal Blues

Please leave the room son
Please go out and play
The baby's still poorly
Been crying all day
The doctor is here
It's not looking good
You can hear the child screaming
In the whole neighbourhood

The ambulance came and it took them away
To a hospital which they call Alder Hey
'She's got meningitis' the auntie did scream
But the mother glazed over as if in a dream
The baby recovered I have to explain
But the mother was never ever the same
'We've got this new treatment for folk like your wife
Electrical waves to eradicate strife
Please sign for it Mister her brain for to jolt
It's sure to transform her this electrical bolt'

Electrical impulses were put through her brain
And the mother was never ever the same

Please leave the room son
Please go out and play
Your mother is poorly
Been crying all day

Love Song

Grandmother Kate was a woman so pure
In spite of the terrible times she endured
Her first six born children all perished and died
Imagine the anguish she felt inside

Different diseases did take them away
Illnesses we don't hear of today
She bore six more children who thank God survived
My dad was the eldest and there's four more (still) alive

She had every reason to question her fate
But she trusted in God and stayed with her faith
She was never embittered and spoke honestly
"My cup is half full not half empty you see"

She prayed for her family at mass every day
For those who survived and those taken away
It makes me so thankful and fills me with pride
That I was her eldest, her first born grandchild

Revered by the neighbours whom she helped all the time
And worshipped by family Grand mother of mine
We loved her so deeply and mourn to this day
This great saintly lady so kind in each way

She was well over ninety when she passed away
Our family still mourn her so needless to say

Edible Message

Our cousin Maureen's got a date
With a bloke called Kenny and she can't wait
But she won't be going very far
'Cause Kenny's gone and smashed his car
So we bought some chips and spelled out on it
'Kenny the car wrecker' on the bonnet
Mo was in an angry state
'Philip and Robert just you wait
Kenny's not happy she said with a frown
Especially when the chips are down'

Blame Song

One Saturday our Robert said
'Let's hide you behind my bed
No one will find you, they'll search every-
where
Your mother will be going spare'

For many hours I sat in gloom
Behind a chair in Robert's room
He brought Jusoda and some sweets
And went to play out in the street

The fun wore out eventually
When all I wanted was a wee
'When will they notice, when will they come
My leg is dead it's gone all numb'

After many hours so it seemed
My dad appeared on the scene
He wasn't half mad he went insane
'It's always me who gets the blame'

Holiday Song

(I wonder if Bob Cook's Shop's still there)

We're going on our holidays
We're going to be free
We're staying at a farmhouse
On the way to Anglesey

We're going in a dormobile
My dad is going to drive (us all mad)
We'll be stuck in a traffic jam
On the old A fifty-five (near Queensferry)

We'll drive through lots of tunnels
Outside of Penmaenmawr
My dad will beep the horn a lot
And we'll know we're not too far

Me dad will drive us round all day
And we will have a laugh
When Uncle Jack who reads the map
Will beat him to the bath

On the farm ....

We'll liberate {terrorise} the animals
And break the country code
We'll leave the gates wide open
So they walk on the road

We'll give to them their 'freedom'
Like Toxteth dogs and cats

The farmer'll tell my father
And he will not like that

We'll go and see our Uncle Bob
Across the Menai Straits
We are his 'favourite' nephews
I bet that he can't wait

We're going to see our cousins
Our Susan and our Jane
Who'll show us round the countryside
Down winding country lanes

We'll run and play in country woods
Until it's nearly dark
It's really rather better
Than a day in Sefton Park

We'll go up to the seaside
To a place called Benlech Bay
It knocks the spots off Otterspool
I'll tell you any day

Then we'll visit Aberfrau
And put our cozzies on
That's where I taught myself to swim
And that's a job well done

It's good to go on Holiday
But great to be back home
And see Bob Cook's shop
In the corner, standing all alone (still there)

Happle Birthday Song

'Come in and have a Happle'
 My Uncle Arthur'd say
But you can't stay for the party
It's Karen's fifth birthday

I know you are both cousins too
And this might sound quite tough
But Robert and young Philip
You like to play too rough

The party is for little girls
With jelly and ice creams
 We don't need you to throw the food
And make the girlie's scream

Now Gillian and Janice
Know just how to play
So come and have a happle
Before you go away

Archie's Song

A boy hung out of the window of an Alt Street tenement flat
'Our Archie's gonna get you, you can be sure of that'
And anyone with any sense ignored this stupid boy
But a certain individual began to get annoyed

'Well go and send your Archie down we'll see what he can do'
'One thing is for certain, he's gonna do for you
Archie's nearly eight feet tall with fists like dynamite
And if I send him down to see you he'll be a fearsome sight

He's beaten Sonny Liston and could outbox Cassius Clay
You don't want to meet our Archie he'll beat you any day
'I'm coming up to get him, I'm gonna sort him out'
As he appeared at the door, he began to shout

'I've come to sort out Archie, that kid's just said he's here
Just send him out to face me, I'll take him have no fear
My Uncle Joe answered the door, 'you've got the wrong house mate
There's no one here called Archie' our Joe did remonstrate'

'But that kid who's at the window said Archie wants a fight
Are you sure you are Archie, you are not a fearsome sight?'
'I'm certainly not Archie, but I'm certainly annoyed
That you have taken notice of a very naughty boy

The idiot, he then backed down, and eventually did go
Leaving me to answer to an angry Uncle Joe

Song for Benny

It's Sunday afternoon at me Grandma's
And all the family's there
But you cannot sit in the corner
That's Uncle Benny's chair.

Uncle Benny's disabled
He lives all my himself
He has a stick for walking
And an iron on his leg.

He's not very keen on children
He dislikes girls and boys
Who are always falling on his leg
And making too much noise.

He doesn't have a telly
So Sunday we must watch
A war film or a western
When they show it on the box.

He dislikes "Pinky and Perky"
Preferring "Call my Bluff"
He goes home about tea time
When he's usually had enough.

He always wears his Sunday best
With highly polished boots
He wears a collar and a tie
And a really smart brown suit.

He wears a lot of Brylcreem
Upon his silver hair
His grooming is immaculate
He dresses with great care.

As for Sunday papers
Suddenly they're gone
Because Benny sits upon them
Til he's read every one

Benny was a seaman
Who fell down a ship's hold
He is me granddad's brother
So he must be getting old.

Benny and me granddad
Were sent to Canada,
Teenage boys out of control
Banished to afar.

There they had adventures
And that's a separate poem
Both of them were seaman
Who worked their ticket home.

Years Later..... .

Benny lived all by himself
But I am proud to say
That me and dad were with him
When Benny passed away.

Song for Joe

My Uncle Joe's a seaman in a uniform so fine
He's a second engineer with the Elder Dempster line,
He wears a neat black blazer with braiding all in gold,
He's been at sea for ages though he isn't very old.

He sails to places far and wide to some not on the map,
And when he comes home on leave he lets me wear his cap.

He writes to Grandma every week which she likes to read
out loud,
He says he's "bored and homesick" but he makes her very
proud.

One time he sailed out to New York and climbed the Empire
State,
He sent a recorded message which we all thought was great.

He brought home discs you can't get here for all the family,
But my dad he kept them for himself he's the eldest one you
see.

He'll bring me home a Parrot, he promised me one day,
And I'm gonna call it Joey, when my uncle sails away.

When I grow up I'll go to sea a sailing I will go,
And I will wear a uniform just like my Uncle Joe.

Angela's Song

My Auntie Angie is a teenager who really
likes Pat Boone
She likes to play her records when I am in
the room,
She stacks them on the Dansette
And they drop down one at a time,
As the arm swings round to play them
And the music sounds just fine.

She's fond of Conway Twitty
And a bloke called Bobby Vee,
But Clarence "Frogman" Henry
Who on earth is he?

It's great to have an auntie
Who's only seventeen,
But it's really time The Beatles
Burst in on the scene.

Poison Dinners

When my mum was poorly, I went to live
 With my wonderful Grandma, but she used
to give
 Me a plateful of cabbage surrounded by
spuds.
"Now come on and eat it, it will do you
good",

"Grandma I love you, but you're not on a
winner
Why do you give me these poisonous dinners"?
"You won't move from that table till you've
eaten that
As for pudding it's goes to the cat" (you
haven't got a cat grandma)

So we both dug our heels in till I eventually
broke
Poisonous dinners, poisonous dinners,
Poisonous dinners make me choke.

First Friend Song

Marie Ellis is a girl
But she plays just like a boy,
And when we play together
It's something of a joy.

She'll scrape her knees like boys do
And climb and drop a wall,
Do all the things a boy can do?
She has no fear at all.

She often stays at Grandma's
She's from the flat upstairs,
There's always fun and laughter
With Marie Ellis there.

She has these smiling friendly eyes
Her hair is short and fair,
I'm really rather lucky
To have a friend like her.

Spoon Song

My Uncle Hal can play the spoons
And 'dish' out quite a 'tasty' tune
When all the familly meet as one
He plays them and we sing along
He bangs them hard against his hand
He's really quite a one man band
Then he'll bang them on his thigh
 And tears will water from one eye
'Cause all this time he'll have a smoke
 It's a wonder that he doesn't choke
And I'm determined that I shall
Play the spoons like Uncle Hal

Cross Purposes

Me Auntie Maureen she's the boss
She taught me how to sign the cross
'In the name of the father and of the son
Down, left and right that's how it's done'

Do know what terrifies me most?
I may be haunted by that (Holy) Ghost

Pier Head Song

We're going to the Pier Head,
We're gonna see some ships
We'll take an orange jubbly
And we'll get a bag of chips

We're gonna take a big green bus
 From Upper Parly Street
And walk down from Mann Island,
That'll save our feet

Me granddad (Troy)'s gonna take us
 And he's a kindly man
He'll probably buy a bag of sweets
Walker's toffees if he can

He's gonna take me cousin
'Cause Robert's going too
We're gonna see some liners
That sail the ocean blue

We may well see a frigate
 Or a yellow submarine
There'll be some tugs and ferry boats,
Some sailors and marines

It's great to live in Liverpool
Or even Birkenhead
'Cause on Saturday and on Sunday,
You can go' the Pier Head

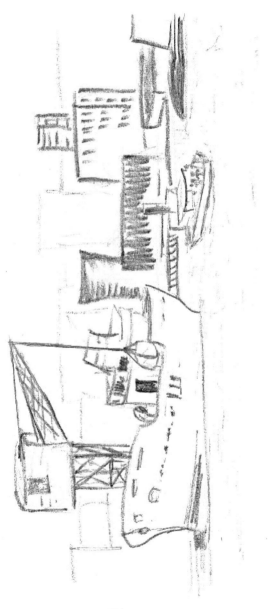

School Songs

First Poem

In St Bernard's school we went to mass
In the middle of the week
To pray to God and Jesus
And penitence to seek
The mass was said in Latin
And therefore we would pray
For Dominic for biscuits (et cum spiritu tuo)
And that woman Agnes Day
The altar boys were from our class
But never ever me
My (maternal) Grandma was a protestant
Not in the rules you see
Or perhaps I was a naughty boy
And messed around in class
And when the priest did turn his back
I messed around in mass

St Bernard's church quite near our home
Was where I wrote my very first poem
I wrote it all in pencil
Upon a column tall
But for this very naughty boy
The writing was on the wall

It went" Ding Dong bell pussy's in the well
Who put him in? Father Flynn "

"You bold boy Philip Domingo, woe betide your soul
You'll burn in Satan's kitchen, you'll sizzle on his coal "

"Excuse me Mrs Revie
How do you know it's me?"
You're the only boy
Who'd dare to write
Such rubbish poetry!"

Obligation Song

Today is the feast of St. Peter and Paul,
It's called obligation but there's no school at all,
It's good to be Catholic on a day like today
Because once you've done mass you are free and away,
To laugh at the kids down in the Tiber Street school,
Who labour in class as they follow the rules,
I swear I heard clearly one of them say
"It would be good to be Catholic on a day like today"

We would go into town or to Old Pier Head
Or play "kick the can" down in Alt Street instead,
There is more to being Catholic than a day out of class,
Like every Sunday you must go to mass (not to mention con-
fession, Benediction etc),
But we're free for the day so we won't complain
And think of the Tiber Street kids – such a shame,
We may go to the park for a game of football,
Thank God for St. Peter and for St. Paul.

Rule Song

Sister John applies the rules
To children at St. Bernard's School,
And for a nun she's very stern
And keen that all the pupils learn.

To read and write and worship God
She rules it with an iron rod,
And if you fail to understand
She applies the ruler to your hand.

And I would often dwell upon
The thought of a woman known as "John",
And later wondered if she knew
That somewhere was a 'boy named Sue?'.

Mass Exodus

We must hold hands on the way to church
Down the labyrinthine streets,
In a line they call a crocodile
With sixty children's feet,
We'll mingle with the shoppers
As we wind down Lodge Lane,
And get our balaclavas wet
As we walk in the rain,
I might see me mum in Benson's (chemist)
Or in the Maypole store
That's where she does the shopping
I'll see her there for sure.

We're going to Benediction
With a priest called Father Flynn,
Who talks to us in Latin
Then we sing lots of hymns,
There's one about sacrament
And one called "Have Maria",
We'd rather sing "She Loves You"
As The Beatles are "the gear",

The priest he says's a few more prayers
And he becomes intense,
He swings around this golden orb
Which lets off some incense,
The smoke was getting rather thick
There was choking in the choir,

And a boy we know shouts "Father Flynn
your handbags gone on fire".

Our Lady of Lourdes and St. Bernard's Church Kingsley Road

Chanting the Tables

Once two is two,
Two twos are four,
When the lesson's over,
I'm flying through the door.

Three twos are six,
Four twos are eight,
When the school day's over,
I'm flying through the gate.

Five twos are ten,
Six twos are more,
Soon I'm playing football,
A goal or two to score.

Seven twos are fourteen,
Eight twos are not,
Soon we're playing "kick the can",
A game we like a lot.

Nine twos are eighteen,
Ten twos a score,
When the lesson's over,
I'm flying through the door.

Permission Song

Please can I go to the toilet miss?
I think I'm going to burst,
I'm surely going to wet myself
Or maybe something worse,
I have been holding on since break
I really need to go,
I know you don't allow it
But it's urgent now you know.

Please can I go to the toilet miss?
I cannot concentrate,
On things like long division
Remainders they can wait,
It will be so embarrassing
A thought beyond belief,
Oh hang these damned gerzzinter sums
And give me some relief.

CORONATION SONG
(song for Barbara)

Because we're making so much noise
All the girl's must sit by boys,
For me it's worked out for the best
Because now I sit with Barbara West,
Whose hair's in ringlets not just curls
The prettiest of all the girls.

Now learning will become a joy
Because she's more fun than any boy,
I'll help her do her "take aways"
And we can chat away all day,
Then I can dream that she will be
Just as keen on this as me.

I'll marry Barbara, one day, maybe
The girl they chose to crown Our Lady.

Topical Songs

Doorstep Vigil

The mothers of our street gathered around our step
And read about those murders unashamedly they wept
"How could she let him do it that very wicked man
She's as bad as he is to take part in the plan"

All the Exe Street mothers were beside themselves with grief
When they read about the torture and sins beyond belief
"What's the matter mother why are you so blue?"
"They've murdered little children similar to you"

She must be very evil the mothers all agreed
To stand there and not help them, to countenance the deed
It could have been our children it fills us full of fear
The Moors are near to Manchester and that's not far from
here

I think of little Lesley Ann her little face I see
I thought, "She's only ten years old, My God that could be
me"
Yes the mothers of Exe Street wept freely on our step
An image so indelible not easy to forget

Cavern Song

They're going to the Cavern
The hottest place in town,
They're going to hear the latest groups
In a cellar full of sound.

They may get to see the Mersey Beats
And other famous acts,
The place it will be heaving
The cellar will be packed.

A sheet of condensation
Will run right down the wall,
And as for conversations
You won't hear those at all.

One time they saw "The Beatles"
Whom everyone adored,
They're going to the Cavern
If not, "The Iron Door".

They're going to the Cavern
Which they all think is great,
But we can never join them
Because we're only eight.

Bad Tidings over Good Hidings

Why are 'hidings so damn good
I've never really understood
Why do they cause such great alarm
When they never do you any harm

Why does the stench of 'healthy' fear
So pollute the atmosphere
Why does it hurt you, more than me?
Surely that's insanity

Why are we bound to spoil a child
If we spare the rod and beatings vile
Why are 'hidings' so damn good
Please explain I wish you would

Boots of Thunder

A tribute to the late great Billy Liddell and the man who worshipped him from the Kop.

When I was born in fifty-five, the greatest hero then alive?
The Scotsman with the boots of thunder, which tore defences well asunder.
Upon the wing he played the game, and Billy Liddell was his name.

It was an April Saturday – Liverpool at Leeds away,
When midwives did deliver me, at Oxford Street maternity.
"A baby boy – we've got a lad, " my mother did inform my dad,
"I'm thrilled to bits but can I tell you that Billy Liddell's just scored two.
Against Leeds United's centre-half, none other than the great John Charles".
The earliest words I learned to say, not nursery rhymes, no "curds and whey".
But "Liddellpool, Hip, Hip, Hooray!"
And so we were to live our lives,
from three o'clock till quart' to five,
Endless Saturdays to endure, dependent on a football score.

Upon the mantelpiece at home, there stood a picture quite alone,
Cloven hair-style, parted down the middle, above the craggy smile of.........Billy Liddell.
Of Billy's praises dad did sing, at centre-forward and the wing,

"William Beveridge", he would enthuse. "Played for Great Britain with Matthews.
What an honour – and what is nice, the only two selected twice!".

It's Manchester City in the cup, we're two-one down, time nearly up,
An equalising shot then flew, just as the final whistle blew.
So Billy's goal was disallowed, in spite of protests from the crowd.
                (and one man in particular!).

At Goodison with Uncle Stan, who is an Evertonian,
                (no known cure)
Billy L. and Johnny Evans took my dad to seventh heaven.
As Liverpool from Division Two humiliated boys in blue.
Come on Toffees what's the score? Blue boys NIL Red men FOUR.

Now my own heroes come and go, comparisons they start to flow.
"What about Roger Hunt, St. John?"
"No match for the chosen one. "
"And Kevin Keegan does he impress?"
"No candle held to the Scots' Express".
"And Kenny the Aristocat?"
------------------------Silence--------------------
"Philip, please don't make me answer that".

It's 1980 in the rain, near the Players' Entrance before a game.
Just as we are to take our place, my dad spots a familiar face,
"Look it's Billy, there's no doubt".

"Say hello dad but please don't shout".
"Hello Billy how are you?"
He smiled politely, "Fine thank you".
But do you know what is really sad?

.... He never recognised my dad. (Why should he?)

As Billy approaches St. Peter's gates, a crowd has gathered and guess who waits.
Right at the front to greet the man? It's my old dad his greatest fan.
And he will take Billy by the hand and show him to his seat in the heavenly stand.

My big regret right to this day is never seeing Billy play.

"Too Song"

Too young to be a rocker, too young to be a mod,
Too bad to be a Catholic and you must believe in God,
Too clean to be a hippy, too straight to be a gay,
Too young to have a girlfriend to prove it anyway,
Too poor for a Ben Sherman and it's legendary pleat,
The shirt I always wanted to parade in our old street,
Too young to worship Elvis, too naughty to like Cliff,
But I'm turned on to Keith Richards, when he plays demonic riffs,
Too young for Jimi Hendrix who died on me too soon,
But old enough to like Pink Floyd and "The dark side of the Moon",
Too macho to fancy T. Rex, white Swans are not for me,
Give me Zeppelin any day and the band they call "The Free".

Anthem for the Fallen Youth

In Aberfan no poppies grow
But hearts still bleed, a constant flow,
The slurry mountain came one day
And took, en masse, the youth away,
The tiny school at mountain side
Submerged in seconds, a hundred died.

In valleys deep, they pray for souls
Of the generation lost to coal.
And older people pay respect
To their lost young, slain by neglect.
The guilty coal board now all dead
With burning coals, they made their bed.
In Aberfan the people weep
"With miles to go before they sleep".

End Song

Demolition Song

As the sign went up on the telegraph pole
The women gathered round
"They're going to move our families
And knock the houses down
We'll get an inside toilet
And a garden for the kids (a good swap)
But what about Nan and Grandad
Where are they going to live?"

As the neighbours went for offers
For Hough Green and Halewood
My dad said "we want Allerton
Those new estates are not so good"

Mum said "I want a brand new house
Like those in Cantril Farm"
But Dad stood firm for Allerton
"Those old houses have such charm
 The area is well established too
I've got some friends out there
The bus route's good
There's lots of parks and trees most every-
where"

And as folks moved out in dribs and drabs
A proud community
Was turned into a ghetto
A self fulfilling prophecy

Daily Telegraph Saturday July 9th 2005

The birthplace of Ringo Starr, the former Beatle, could be demolished as a result of a re-generation scheme aproved by Liverpool council yeserday.
In the face of vigorous opposition.
The Victorian terrace house in Madryn Street, Toxteth, is one of 460 properties ear-marked for demolition under a government backed new heartland scheme.
The city councils decision prompted Lord Alton, the former Liverpool MP. and crossbench peer, to accuse the Government and the council of having "learnt nothing" from the "disastrous" demolition schemes of the 1960s, which "uprooted communities"

Acknowledgements

Many thanks to John Emmerson and his staff at Birkenhead Press for having faith in me and giving me a chance. Also to John Pearman at 'Red All Over the Land' for first seeing something in my work. To my wife Jo. for being as honestly critical as only a wife can be. To my sister Gillian for encouragement and showing an interest. To cousin Maureen for the same and giving me the idea about the washhouse. To cousin Michael for giving me extra information on Uncle Benny To Peter and Katherine for putting up with my ramblings at home. To Lorna Clarke at K. C. C. Northampton for typing up many files. To friends and colleagues at K. C. C. for encouragement Irmgard, Alison, and most notably Sue Lomas who said my stuff was 'interesting'-praise indeed. To others who have encouraged also such as John and Liz Buckell. And also to my Godson Tim who said it was 'wicked'. I presume that is positive. And not least to Terry for finally agreeing to illustrate and putting it into perspective by telling me he had played in houses that had been bombed 'that' day.

In addition I would like to acknowledge the influences of my teachers and lecturers who imbued in me a love of the written word. Most notably Mr Keogh at St Bernards School, Mr Hartley at Cardinal Allen, Messrs. Burns and McHugh at De La Salle, Barry Maybury and the wonderful Dr. Mary McGowan at Shenstone New College Worcestershire. Whichever world you are in now. Thanks!